Broken to Build Journal

Transforming Your Journal Into a Captivating Book

Crystal C. Love

Edited by
Nicole Queen

To those who have ever felt broken or silenced, this journal is for you.
May your words become a bridge to healing and restoration as you share your truth.

"I now rejoice in my sufferings for you, and fill up in my flesh what is lacking in the afflictions of Christ, for the sake of His body, which is the church,"

— Colossians 1:24 NKJV

"Now I rejoice in my sufferings on your behalf. And with my own body I supplement whatever is lacking [on our part] of Christ's afflictions, on behalf of His body, which is the church."

— Colossians 1:24 AMP

Contents

Introduction

Have you ever felt like there's a story inside of you— one that's waiting to be told? Perhaps it's a story of overcoming challenges, finding hope in the midst of brokenness, or sharing wisdom and lessons you've learned along the way. Writing a book is a powerful way to give voice to your experiences, inspire others, and leave a lasting impact. The *Broken to Building: Book Project Journal* is here to guide you step by step through that process.

I created this workbook journal because I know what it feels like to have a vision, but struggle when it comes to seeing it through. I remember the moment I released my first book, *Finding Normal: Breaking Free from Culture Shock*. It was a major accomplishment for me. Writing that book was about discovering my voice, sharing my truth, and trusting God to use my story to help others.

So, if you're holding this journal in your hands, it means you, too, have a story to share, a message to write, and a purpose to fulfill. You may not know where to start, and that's okay. This journal will help you build your book one step at a time—starting with your *why*, creating your chapters, and reflecting on what matters most.

Here's what you can expect as you journey through this journal:

- A clear structure to help you organize your ideas and write with intention
- Prompts and reflections to guide you through each chapter and section

- Encouragement to explore your past, embrace your truth, and trust God's plan for your writing

Writing a book can feel like a big task, but you don't have to do it alone. I invite you to take this journey with courage, faith, and an open heart. Let God guide you as you write, reflect, and build something beautiful out of what was once broken.

Let's begin.

How to Use This Book

The journey to writing a book is about uncovering your truth, reflecting on your experiences, and sharing your story in a way that impacts others. Here's how to get the most out of this journal:

1. Start With Prayer and Reflection

Before you begin writing, take time to pause, pray, and ask God for guidance. This book is about more than just telling your story—it's about writing with purpose. Create a quiet atmosphere where you can reflect and meditate, whether in silence or with soft music. Use this time to ask:

- *What message does God want me to share?*
- *Who is this book for?*
- *How will my story impact others?*

2. Work Step by Step

The journal is structured to guide you through the writing process one section at a time:

Front Matter

- Endorsements

- Dedication
- Epigraph
- Table of Contents
- Foreword
- Preface

Body Matter

- Introduction
- Chapters

Back Matter

- Afterword
- Acknowledgments
- Appendix/ Resources
- About the Author

3. Write Consistently and Creatively

Writing a book doesn't have to feel overwhelming. Here are a few tips to keep the process manageable and enjoyable:

- *Set a Daily Goal:* Commit to writing for 30 minutes a day or setting a word count goal. Small, consistent efforts lead to big results.

- *Allow Yourself to Be Vulnerable:* Writing your book may require revisiting past experiences or challenging moments. Embrace this as part of your growth. God often uses our brokenness to build something beautiful.

- *Capture Your Ideas Freely:* Don't overthink or edit while you write. Use this journal to pour your thoughts onto the page. Editing and refining come later.

4. Use Reflection Prompts to Stay on Track

Throughout this journal, you'll find prompts and tips to guide you. Use these questions as checkpoints to help clarify your message, inspire your next chapter, or deepen your writing. If you feel stuck, go back to these prompts or spend time in prayer for fresh direction.

5. Lean on Resources and Support

You are not alone in this process. Feel free to reach out to me for additional support, or connect with any of the individuals mentioned in this journal who are ready to assist you on your journey. Don't ever give up on yourself. Trust that your story matters, too, and your voice will reach those who need it most.

* * *

This journal is your safe space—a place to write, create, and discover. Don't rush the process. Give yourself permission to write imperfectly, to reflect deeply, and to trust that every word is part of a bigger purpose.

Your journey from "broken" to "build" begins here, and I am cheering you on as you share your story with the world. You've got this—but most importantly, God's got you!

Happy Writing!

Part One

Front Matter

The *front matter* contains the introductory sections of a book that appear before the main content begins. These sections provide important information and set the stage for the reader's experience.

Endorsements

Endorsements are testimonials or recommendations from notable individuals, authors, or experts that can vouch for the quality and value of a book. These endorsements can enhance credibility and attract potential readers.

Example Endorsement

 Broken to Build masterfully delves into the divine process of experiencing brokenness in order to be rebuilt stronger in faith and character. Drawing from the author's journey, this transformative book serves as a beacon of hope, guiding readers to embrace their brokenness as a pathway to healing, wholeness, and accelerated spiritual growth in God.

— Archbishop R. L. Dennis, *Kingdom Fellowship Covenant Ministries*

* * *

Think of individuals who can vouch for the value of your message—mentors, peers, or respected voices in your field. Reach out and gather their words of support to strengthen your book's impact.

List the names of the individuals you've identified, along with their contact information:

Contact Name: _____ Phone/ Email: _____

Contact Name: _____ Phone/ Email: _____

Contact Name: _____ Phone/ Email: _____

Contact Name: _____ Phone/ Email: _____

Contact Name: _____ Phone/ Email: _____

Contact Name: _____ Phone/ Email: _____

Contact Name: _____ Phone/ Email: _____

Contact Name: _____ Phone/ Email: _____

Contact Name: _____ Phone/ Email: _____

Contact Name: _____ Phone/ Email: _____

Contact Name: _____ Phone/ Email: _____

Contact Name: _____ Phone/ Email: _____

Contact Name: _____ Phone/ Email: _____

Contact Name: _____ Phone/ Email: _____

Contact Name: _____ Phone/ Email: _____

Contact Name: _____ Phone/ Email: _____

Contact Name: _____ Phone/ Email: _____

Dedication

The *dedication page* is where you pay tribute to someone special or significant in your life. It shows gratitude and recognition for their support or influence.

How to Write It

1. *Choose who to dedicate it to.* Think about the person or people who have made a difference in your life or your writing journey.

2. *Write a simple phrase or a page* to express your genuine and heartfelt thank you for what they have done.

Example Dedication

 To my parents, whose unwavering support has guided me every step of the way. Thank you for believing in my dreams and encouraging me to share my story with the world.

* * *

Take a moment to reflect and dedicate this book to someone who has inspired or supported you. Write down your thoughts.

_____

_____

_____

_____

_____

_____

_____

_____

_____

_____

_____

_____

_____

_____

_____

_____

_____

_____

_____

_____

_____

_____

_____

_____

_____

_____

_____

_____

_____

_____

Epigraph

An *epigraph* is a short quotation, phrase, or excerpt placed at the beginning of a book, chapter, or section. It is often chosen to set the tone, provide insight, or highlight a theme relevant to the content that follows. Epigraphs can come from literature, poetry, religious texts, speeches, or even original sayings.

Example Epigraph

 We are hard pressed on every side, but not crushed; perplexed, but not in despair.

— 2 Corinthians 4:8

* * *

Take a moment to consider a relevant quote, scripture, or excerpt that can engage readers, spark reflection, and provide context before introducing the main content. Jot down some ideas on the following page.

Table of Contents

The *Table of Contents* provides a clear overview of the book. It helps readers navigate through the chapters and find specific topics of interest easily.

How to Create It

1. List all the chapters. Write down the titles of each chapter in the order they appear.

2. Include subsections (optional). If your chapters have subsections or major topics, this gives the readers more detail to help them locate specific information quickly.

3. *Page numbers* allow readers to find the sections they want to read without flipping through the entire book.: Add the corresponding page numbers next to each chapter title.

Table of Contents Example

Chapter Layout Example #1: Places of Brokenness

Consider organizing your book into 5-8 chapters, each focusing on a specific theme or experience of brokenness. Within each chapter, include 4-8 pages that offer space for writing, reflections, or exercises, resulting in a total of 20-64 pages.

Chapter Layout Example #2: Places of Testimony and Victory

Similarly, you can structure this section with 5-8 chapters, each containing 4-8 pages, for a total of 20-64 pages.

Conclusion Chapter (Epilogue)

Wrap up your book with 1-2 pages of final thoughts, reflections, and words of encouragement for the reader.

Reflection Pages

After each chapter, include a few pages to encourage personal reflection and help readers process their experiences (10-20 pages total).

* * *

Jot down your ideas for organizing your chapters, including potential chapter titles.

_____

_____

_____

_____

_____

_____

_____

_____

_____

_____

_____

_____

_____

_____

_____

_____

_____

_____

_____

_____

_____

_____

_____

_____

_____

_____

_____

_____

_____

_____

Foreword

A *foreword* is an introductory section written by someone other than the author, typically a respected figure in the field related to the book's subject. It provides context for the book and often highlights the author's qualifications and the importance of the book's content.

Example Foreword

In *Broken to Build*, Crystal Love invites readers to see brokenness as a transformative journey toward healing and renewal. Drawing from personal experiences and scriptural insights, she highlights God's promise in Jeremiah 18:4, reminding us that brokenness can lead to beauty. Her reflections align with Paul's words in 2 Corinthians 12:9, emphasizing that God's grace shines brightest in our weaknesses. Through powerful anecdotes and biblical teachings from Ecclesiastes 3:1 to Isaiah 58:8, Crystal encourages us to embrace our own processes of healing and rebuilding, making this book a life-changing journey toward abundance guided by.

* * *

Identify respected figures in the field related to your book who can also enhance your credibility. Reach out to see if they'd be willing to write your foreword. Typically, you'll only need one individual for this.

List the names of the individuals you've identified, along with their contact information:

Contact Name: _____ Phone/ Email: _____

Contact Name: _____ Phone/ Email: _____

Contact Name: _____ Phone/ Email: _____

Contact Name: _____ Phone/ Email: _____

Contact Name: _____ Phone/ Email: _____

Contact Name: _____ Phone/ Email: _____

Contact Name: _____ Phone/ Email: _____

Contact Name: _____ Phone/ Email: _____

Contact Name: _____ Phone/ Email: _____

Contact Name: _____ Phone/ Email: _____

Contact Name: _____ Phone/ Email: _____

Contact Name: _____ Phone/ Email: _____

Contact Name: _____ Phone/ Email: _____

Contact Name: _____ Phone/ Email: _____

Contact Name: _____ Phone/ Email: _____

Preface

A *preface* is an introductory section of a book written by the author, usually placed before the main content. It provides readers with insight into the book's creation, purpose, and context. Unlike the introduction, which sets up the content of the book for readers, the preface often focuses on the author's personal journey, inspiration, or motivation for writing the book.

Example Preface (Sample Paragraph)

 In writing this book, I wanted to share my journey of overcoming brokenness and finding purpose. These pages reflect years of experiences, prayers, and lessons I've learned along the way. My hope is that this book becomes a guide for those navigating their own paths to healing.

* * *

Take a moment to consider what additional insights you'd like to share about your book. Include your thoughts on the following page.

Part Two

Body Matter

The *body matter* refers to the main content of a book—the core material that delivers the message, story, or information the author intends to share. It is the largest part of the book, following the front matter and preceding the back matter.

Introduction

The *introduction* sets the stage for your book. It explains why you wrote it and what readers can expect to learn or experience while reading and after they finish it.

How to Write It

1. *What is your why?* Begin with a quote, a personal story, or a thought-provoking question to grab your reader's attention.

   - Example: "Have you ever felt lost in a world where you feel like you don't belong?"

2. *What is your purpose?* Explain to your readers why you wrote this book. Who and/ or what inspired you? What message do you want to convey?

   - Example: "This book is my journey of overcoming my failures and discovering my true self amidst the chaos."

3. *Explain what to expect.* Briefly describe what the book covers. Give a sample of the topics and different themes you may want to discuss.

- Example: "In the chapters ahead, I will share Biblical principles, as well as my personal experiences, that may help you navigate through your own challenges."

4. *Invite the reader in.* Encourage readers to engage with the writing and reflect on their own experiences, while reading.

- Example: "I invite you to join me on this journey and discover how you, too, can find your *normal*."

* * *

Start drafting your introduction by sharing your *why*— the purpose behind your book, who it's for, and what readers can expect to gain. Use this section to set the tone, engage your audience, and invite them into your story.

_____
_____
_____
_____
_____
_____
_____
_____
_____
_____
_____
_____
_____
_____
_____
_____
_____
_____
_____

Chapter 1

Chapter Title: _____

_____

_____

_____

_____

_____

_____

_____

_____

_____

_____

_____

_____

_____

_____

_____

_____

_____

_____

Chapter 2

Chapter Title: _____

_____

_____

_____

_____

_____

_____

_____

_____

_____

_____

_____

_____

_____

_____

_____

_____

_____

_____

_____

Chapter 3

Chapter Title: _____

_____

_____

_____

_____

_____

_____

_____

_____

_____

_____

_____

_____

_____

_____

_____

_____

_____

Chapter 4

Chapter Title: _____

_____

_____

_____

_____

_____

_____

_____

_____

_____

_____

_____

_____

_____

_____

_____

_____

_____

_____

_____

_____

_____

Chapter 5

Chapter Title: _____

_____

_____

_____

_____

_____

_____

_____

_____

_____

_____

_____

_____

_____

_____

_____

_____

_____

_____

_____

_____

Chapter 6

Chapter Title: _____

_____
_____
_____
_____
_____
_____
_____
_____
_____
_____
_____
_____
_____
_____
_____
_____
_____
_____
_____

Chapter 7

Chapter Title: _____

_____

_____

_____

_____

_____

_____

_____

_____

_____

_____

_____

_____

_____

_____

_____

_____

_____

_____

_____

Chapter 8

Chapter Title: _____

_____

_____

_____

_____

_____

_____

_____

_____

_____

_____

_____

_____

_____

_____

_____

_____

_____

_____

_____

Part Three

Back Matter

The *back matter* refers to the sections of a book that appear after the main content (body matter) has concluded. It provides additional information, resources, and acknowledgments that enhance the reader's experience or offer further value.

Afterword

An *afterword* is a reflective section that typically appears at the end of a book and is often written by the author or an expert in the field. It may discuss the book's impact, address further developments in the subject matter, or provide additional insights that enhance the reader's understanding.

Example Afterword (Sample Paragraph)

In "Finding Normal," Crystal Love offers a refreshing take on life's chaos and our desire for stability, resonating with anyone longing for a sense of "normal." Her candid exploration reveals that our understanding of normal may need reevaluating. By sharing her journey, she shows that both joy and struggle are essential to our stories, reminding us that life's ups and downs are inherently normal. If you find yourself at a crossroads, this book will inspire you to view chaos as a beautiful version of normal.

Sean Gresh
Author, Becoming a Father (Bantam Books)
Adjunct Professor, Northeastern University,
College of Professional Studies

* * *

Identify experts in the field related to your book. Reach out to see if they'd be willing to write your afterword. Typically, you'll only need one individual for this.

List the names of the individuals you've identified, along with their contact information:

Contact Name: _____ Phone/ Email: _____

Contact Name: _____ Phone/ Email: _____

Contact Name: _____ Phone/ Email: _____

Contact Name: _____ Phone/ Email: _____

Contact Name: _____ Phone/ Email: _____

Contact Name: _____ Phone/ Email: _____

Contact Name: _____ Phone/ Email: _____

Contact Name: _____ Phone/ Email: _____

Contact Name: _____ Phone/ Email: _____

Contact Name: _____ Phone/ Email: _____

Contact Name: _____ Phone/ Email: _____

Contact Name: _____ Phone/ Email: _____

Contact Name: _____ Phone/ Email: _____

Contact Name: _____ Phone/ Email: _____

Contact Name: _____ Phone/ Email: _____

Contact Name: _____ Phone/ Email: _____

Contact Name: _____ Phone/ Email: _____

Acknowledgments

The *Acknowledgments* section is where you express your gratitude to those who contributed to your writing journey. This may include individuals who provided support, guidance, feedback, or inspiration.

How to Write It

List key contributors. Mention anyone who played a significant role, such as mentors, family, friends, or colleagues.

Example Acknowledgments (Sample Section)

> I want to thank my parents for their endless encouragement and love throughout this journey. Special thanks to my mentor, Dr. Smith, whose invaluable feedback and guidance helped me shape my ideas into a coherent narrative. I'm also grateful to my friends who patiently listened to my thoughts and cheered me on.

* * *

Take some time to identify everyone who has supported in some way. Write down their names and your message of acknowledgment to them.

_____

_____

_____

_____

_____

_____

_____

_____

_____

_____

_____

_____

_____

_____

_____

_____

_____

_____

_____

_____

_____

_____

_____

_____

_____

_____

_____

_____

_____

_____

Appendix/ Resources

The *Appendix/ Resources* section provides readers with additional materials, references, or tools related to the topics discussed in the book. This can enhance their understanding or help them delve deeper into the subject matter.

How to Write It

1. *List relevant material.* Include books, articles, websites, or organizations that relate to your book's themes.

2. *Categorize your resources, if needed.* If you have multiple types of resources, consider organizing them into sections (e.g., Books, Websites, Support Organizations) for easier navigation.

Example Resources Section
(Books)

- *Finding Normal: Living Free from Culture Shock* by Crystal Love – (A transformative guide that offers practical strategies and insights)

- *I'm Breaking Down to Build Up* by Crystal Love — (A powerful narrative that explores personal growth)

(Websites)

- www.crystallove-theauthor.com (A resource for readers to learn more about personal development)
- www.holisticministrieslove.com (Offers support and resources for individuals seeking holistic well-being)

Support Organizations

- Emerging Voices Consulting & Solutions – Provides coaching and consultancy for individuals and organizations
- Vision Publishing House– A platform that supports visionary voices (leaders, organizations, and brands) with writing and publishing assistance through their signature "speaking" method

How to Develop Your Resource Section

(Books)

- "[Book Title]"by [Author Name] – [Brief Description of Book– focus on themes and insights offered.]
- "[Book Title]" by [Author Name] – [Brief Description of Book – emphasize personal growth and challenges addressed.]

(Websites)

- [Website](http://www.example.com) – [Description of Website – what resources and information can be found here.]
- [Website](http://www.example.com) – [Description of Website – what resources and information can be found here.]

(Support Organizations)

- [Organization Name]– [Brief description of what the organization offers, its focus, and how it helps individuals or groups.]

- [Organization Name]– [Brief description of what the organization offers, its focus, and how it helps individuals or groups.]

* * *

Consider including supplemental resources that complement your book's topic to enhance your readers' understanding. Jot down your ideas below.

_____

_____

_____

_____

_____

_____

_____

_____

_____

_____

_____

_____

_____

_____

_____

_____

_____

_____

_____

_____

_____

_____

_____

About the Author

The *About the Author* section is a brief biography typically included at the end of a book, often within the back matter. It introduces readers to the author, highlighting their background, expertise, and accomplishments. This section provides context for why the author is qualified to write on the book's subject and allows readers to connect with the author on a more personal level.

About the Author Example

[Author Name] is an accomplished writer, speaker, and [profession]. With a passion for empowering others, [she/he/they] draws from personal experiences and professional expertise to inspire readers to embrace healing and purpose. [Author Name] is also the author of *[Other Book Title]*, and their work has been featured in [notable publications or platforms]. When not writing, [Author Name] enjoys [personal hobbies or activities]. Learn more at [website] or connect on social media: @[handle].

* * *

Start writing your author bio to include in your book, and consider adding a professional photo to accompany this section.

Final Thoughts

As you close this workbook journal, remember that every word you've written brings you one step closer to completing your book and sharing your story with the world. Writing is about courageously sharing your voice, inspiring others, and leaving a lasting impact.

Trust the process, believe in the power of your message, and know that what you are creating has purpose. God has equipped you for this journey, and your words matter. Keep writing, keep building, and never underestimate the lives you will touch through your story.

Your journey is just beginning, and the world is waiting to hear from you.

Finish strong— you've got this!

About the Author

Crystal Love, a native of Baltimore, is a dedicated mother, Elder, and Prophet within the Christian community. She committed her life to the Lord in 1997 at the age of 17 and was called to ministry at 20. With 25 years of ministry experience, Crystal currently serves as an Elder at Kingdom Worship Center in Baltimore, MD, under the leadership of Bishop Gregory Dennis and Pastor Tonya Dennis.

Passionate about community service, Crystal volunteers in homeless shelters, teaches at women's transitional homes, engages in outreach and evangelism, and hosts empowerment events aimed at uplifting and encouraging individuals to walk in their God-given callings. In 2011, she founded Holistic Ministries, focusing on addressing the comprehensive needs of individuals—spiritual, emotional, social, and physical. Holistic Ministries, Inc. is a parachurch affiliate of Kingdom Fellowship Covenant Ministries, Inc., under the leadership of her spiritual father, Archbishop Ralph Dennis.

An author of several books that promote healing and wholeness, Crystal holds a Bachelor's degree in Pastoral Counseling, equipping her to help others recover through the power of the Holy Spirit. She is currently pursuing a Bachelor of Science degree with a focus on Religion and Christian Leadership & Ministries. Her ministry reflects her deep commitment to helping individuals discover their purpose in Jesus Christ and further expand the Kingdom of God.

 *"When Jesus saw him lie, and knew that he had been now a long time in that case, he saith unto him, Wilt thou be made whole?"*

—John 5:6

Be sure to purchase your copy of the "Broken to Build" Bible Study Curriculum & 30-Day Devotional

For more books and updates:

🌐 crystallove-theauthor.com

✉ hello@crystallove-theauthor.com

f facebook.com/crystal_love

🐦 twitter.com/crystalcauthor

📷 instagram.com/holisticministrieslove